BODHIDHARMA

STILL UNKNOWN

DR. RIYA

BODHIDHARMA

THIS BOOK NAMED 'BODHIDHARMA' IS DEDICATED TO THE PERSON WHO WAS NOT ONLY AN ANCIENT BUDDHIST MONK BUT ALSO THE FIRST INDIAN DOCTOR & SCIENTIST TO WENT TO FOREIGN COUNTRY & TO PROMOTE HIS TREATMENTS, RESEARCHES, MARTIAL ARTS, HYPNOTISM & ZEN TEACHINGS. HE WAS A GREAT VAIDYA. AT MANY PLACES, IN CHINA, JAPAN & THAILAND, HE IS PRAISED AS GOD, BUT MOST OF WE INDIANS ARE STILL UNAWARE ABOUT THIS INDIAN VAIDYA. EVEN HIS, BIGGEST STATUE IS TOO LOACTED AT DAMO LAKE, IN CHINA. BUT, DO WE KNOW WHO IS HE? WHY THEY PRAISE HIM?

LET'S STUDY THIS BOOK TO KNOW ABOUT HIM...

Contents

Foreword

DR. RIYA (BAMS INTERN AT SGC)

I had done my schooling from Sharda Sarvhitkari Model Senior Secondary School, Chandigarh.

I have persued BAMS from Saraswati Ayurveda Hospital & Medical College, Punjab and in the same place doing internship.

In Dec 2020, I had authored Covid & Ayurveda.

Acknowledgements

I WOULD LIKE TO THANK NOTION PRESS FOR PUBLISHING MY BOOK AND GIVING ME SUCH OPPURTUNITY TO SCALE MY BOOK INTO WIDE RANGE OF INDIANS ON NO. 1 VOTED PLATFORM BY INDIAN AUTHORS.

THIS PLATFORM IS BEST SUITED FOR ME TO AWARE THE WHOLE NATION ABOUT BODHIDHARMA.

Prologue

- WITH SPACE REASEARCH, SCIENTISTS SAID WE HAVE 9 PLANETS. THEY HAVE SEEN IT WITH TELESCOPE. BUT, THOUSANDS OF YEARS AGO, IN OUR COUNTRY, PEOPLE PRAYED TO 9 PLANETS. HOW?
- HOW DID ARYA BHATT TOLD US ABOUT EARTH'S RADIUS 1500 YEARS AGO?
- TODAY, IF WE PREDICT RAINS, IT GETS SUNNY. IF WE PREDICT SUNNY DAY, IT RAINS. THIS IS MODERN SCIENCE. BUT, WE CAN EASILY KNOW ABOUT NEW MOON & FULL MOON THAT WOULD COME AFTER 20 YEARS. HOW?
- THIS IS OUR SCIENCE.
- IN 6TH CENTURY, BODHIDHARMA HAD WRITTEN ABOUT EVEN GENETIC SCRIPTURES, RESEARCHES, GENETIC MEMORY, DISORDERS & TREATMENTS TOO.
- TURMERIC- A MEDICINAL HERB FOR ALL DISEASES. APPLYING PASTE OF TURMERIC ALL OVER THE BODY, DO NOT ADDRESS IT AS GOD OR ANY SPIRITUAL MAGIC, INFACT ADDRESS IT AS SCIENCE. IT,S AN ANTIBIOTIC.
- TO PREVENT PESTS IN HOUSE, RANGOLI WAS MADE OF COW-DUNG. BUT NOW, STICKERS ARE USED. WHY?
- NEEM PLANT OUTSIDE HOUSE & BASIL PLANT INSIDE HOUSE, THESE ALL ARE MEDICINAL PLANTS.
- IT'S HIGH TIME TO GAIN KNOWLEDGE ABOUT OUR HISTORIES, CLOSED IN MUSEUMS AT PRESENT TIME. IT'S MUST TO TELL OUR FUTURE GENERATION ABOUT OUR HISTORIES IN MEDICAL SCIENCE ETC...
- THAT'S WHY THIS BOOK IS ABOUT BODHIDHARMA- AN ANCIENT INDIAN MONK & A GREAT VAIDYA.

Bodhidharma Unknown Facts

- BODHIDHARMA WAS AN ANCIENT INDIAN MONK.
- HE WAS A GREAT VAIDYA.
- HE KNEW PECULIARITY OF EACH & EVERY LEAF, AND USE OF EVERY PLANT.
- HE HAD WRITTEN A SCRIPTURE TOO IN WHICH HE HAD MENTIONED ABOUT DIAGNOSIS & TREATMENT OF VARIOUS DISEASES.
- EVEN, HE HAD MENTIONED ABOUT GENETIC CONCEPT, RESEARCHES, DISEASES & TREATMENTS.
- APART FROM BEING A GREAT VAIDYA, HE WAS A GREAT EXPERT IN MARTIAL ARTS & KUNG FU TOO.
- HE WAS THE ONE WHO ORIGINATED KUNG FU IN CHINA WHICH IS NOW MOST PROMINENT IN SHAOLIN TEMPLE IN CHINA.
- HE WAS ALSO AN EXPERT IN SELF DEFENCE.
- HE WAS THE ONE WHO CONSTRUCTED SHAOLIN TEMPLE, THAT'S WHY AT PRESENT HE IS ADDRESSED AS GOD.
- ALONG, WITH ALL THESE, HE WAS ALSO AN EXPERT IN OVERPOWERING OTHERS.
- HE HAD ALSO CONTROL OVER THE FIVE ELEMENTS TOO. HE HAD SUPERNATURAL POWERS.
- EVEN, TODAY,AT PRESENT, MANY PLACES IN CHINA, JAPAN & THAILAND, HE (AN INDIAN) IS ADDRESSED AS GOD & PEOPLE PRAY TO HIM.
- EVEN, HIS BIGGEST STATUE IS TOO LOCATED AT DAMO LAKE, CHINA.
- THE CAVE WHERE HE LIVED IN CHINA, NOW PRESENTLY IS SITUATED IN SHAOLIN TEMPLE SCENIC AREA, DENGFENG CITY, ZHENGZHOU.
- IT REALLY SEEMS SHOCKING, THAT WHOLE ART IN CHINA, JAPAN & THAILAND IS CAME FROM INDIA, THE KNOWLEDGE THAT THEY HAVE ABOUT OUR ANCIENT STUDIES IN DEPTH, THAT WE DOESN,T HAVE. IT'S SO SHAMEFUL FOR US. THAT'S WHY THEY USED TO ATTACK INDIA.
- YOU KNOW, HE WAS AS MUCH AS GOOD AS BUDDHA.

CHAPTER ONE

PALLAV DYNASTY 275CE-897CE

The Pallavas emerged as a formidable power in the South around the 4 th century AD and were at the height of their power in the seventh century AD. They were able to sustain their rule for about 500 years. They built great cities, centres of learning, temples, and sculptures and influenced a large part of Southeast Asia in culture.

Important Facts about Pallavas

- **Who was the founder of the Pallava Dynasty?** There is no clarity on the name of the founder of Pallava dynasty but the rise of Pallavas in the last quarter of the 6th century is attributed to Simha Vishnu.
- **Who was the greatest ruler of the Pallava Dynasty?** Mahendravarman I is considered to be the greatest ruler of the Pallavas. His reign was marked by many architectural and literary achievements which would lay the foundations of future Art and Culture of South India
- **What is the name of the capital of Pallavas?** Kanchipuram was the capital of the Pallavas
- **What are the temples built by Pallavas?** Shore Temple at Mahabalipuram and the Kanchi Kailasanathar Temple at Kanchipuram are famous temples that were constructed during the reign of Pallavas

Political History of Pallavas

- The origins of the Pallavas are shrouded in mystery. There are several theories propounded by historians.
- Some historians say they are a branch of the Parthian people (a tribe from Iran) who gradually migrated to South India.
- Some say they are an indigenous dynasty that arose within the Southern region and were a mix of various tribes.
- Some experts believe them to be of Naga origin who first settled around the Tondaimandalam region near Madras.
- Another theory says that they are descendant from a Chola prince and a Naga princess of Manipallavam (an island off Jaffna, Sri Lanka).
- Some others are of the opinion that the Pallavas were feudatories of the Satavahanas.
- The first Pallava kings ruled during the beginning of the 4th century AD. By the 7th century AD, there were three kingdoms in southern India vying for supremacy namely the Chalukyas of Badami, the Pandyas of Madurai and the Pallavas of Kanchipuram.

The extent of the Pallava dynasty

- The Pallava capital was Kanchipuram.
- Their territories at the height of their powers extended from the northern part of Andhra Pradesh to River Kaveri in the South.
- During the seventh century, the Cholas were reduced to a marginal state by the authority of the Pallavas.
- Vatapi (Badami) was occupied by the Pallava king Narasimhavarman who defeated the Chalukyas.
- The Kalabhra uprising was crushed by the Pandyas, Chalukyas and the Pallavas jointly. The Kalabhras were protesting against the numerous land grants (Brahamadeya) to Brahmanas made by the Brahmanic rulers of the three dynasties.

Rulers of the Pallava Empire

Sivaskanda Varman

- Greatest among the early rulers. Ruled at the beginning of the 4th century AD.
- Performed Ashwamedha and other Vedic sacrifices.

Simhavarman/Simhavishnu

- Was a Buddhist.
- Included Sri Lanka in his kingdom.
- Defeated the contemporary Tamil ruler. Pallava history assumes a definite character from this ruler onwards.

Mahendravarman

- Succeeded Simhavishnu who was his father.
- He was a poet and composed Vichitrachita and Mahavilasa Prahasana.
- He introduced rock-cut temple architecture.
- Was a Jain who converted to Saivism.
- Had on-going rivalry and battles with Pulakesin II of Chalukya dynasty.
- Mahendravarman died in battle with the Chalukyas. He was an able and efficient ruler.

Narasimhavarman I

- Son and successor of Mahendravarman.
- Considered the greatest of the Pallavas. Also called Narasimhavarman Mahamalla/Mamalla.
- Defeated and killed Pulakesin II in 642 AD. He took control of Vatapi, the Chalukya capital and assumed the title 'Vatapikonda'
- Also vanquished the Cholas, Cheras and the Pandyas.
- He sent a naval expedition to Sri Lanka and reinstated the Sinhalese Prince Manivarma.
- He founded the city of Mamallapuram or Mahabalipuram which is named after him.
- Hiuen Tsang visited the Pallava kingdom during his reign in about 640 AD and he describes the people living in his kingdom as happy.
- He also says there was an abundance of agricultural products.
- Great Nayannar saints like Appar, Tirugnanasambandar and Siruthondar lived during his reign.

- He was succeeded by his son Mahendravarman II who ruled from 668 to 670 AD.

Later rulers

- After Mahendravarman II, his son Parameswaravarman became the king.
- During his rule, Kanchipuram was occupied by the Chalukyas.
- Nripatunga was an important king who defeated a Pandya king.
- There were a few other rulers. The last ruler of the Pallava dynasty was Aparajitavarman who was killed in battle with the Cholas.

BODHIDHARMA EARLY LIFE

BIRTH

- HE WAS BORN ON 1 JAN 483CE IN KANCHIPURM, TAMILNADU, INDIA.
- HE WAS A 'SOUTH INDIAN' PRINCE.
- HE WAS BORN IN 'PALLAV DYNASTY' OF SOUTHERN REGION.
- HE WAS THE 3RD CHILD OF PALLAV KING 'SUGANDAN'.
- HE WAS A 'KSHATRIYA'.

YOUNG LIFE

- SINCE AGE OF 7, HE WAS INTERESTED IN LORD BUDDHA'S TEACHINGS.
- HE WAS HIS FATHER'S FAVOURITE SON, THAT MADE HIS ELDER BROTHERS JEALOUS.
- IN FEAR THAT THEIR FATHER WOULD GIVE THRONE TO BODHIDHARMAN, THEY TRIED TO KILL HIM TOO, BUT THEY FAILED EACH TIME.
- ON ACCOUNT OF THAT INCIDENTS, BODHIDHARMA LEFT POLITICS, AND, WENT AWAY FROM HOME TO STUDY BUDDHISM.

- HE STUDIED BUDDHISM WITH 'PRAJANTARA', WHO WAS THE GREAT BUDDHIST TEACHER & CAME TO KANCHIPURAM ESPECIALLY ON INVITATION OF KING TO TEACH HIS SON BODHIDHARMA.
- BODHIDHARMA STUDIED FROM PRAJANTARA SINCE HER DEATH.
- BEFORE, SHE DIED, SHE TOLD HIM TO GO TO CHINA TO SPREAD THE TEACHINGS OF LORD BUDDHA.

MARRIAGE LIFE

- HE MARRIED TO ABHINAYA
- HE HAD TWO SONS
- HE WENT OUT FOR CHINA, LEAVING BEHIND HIS WIFE AND SONS.

CHAPTER THREE

BODHIDHARMA LATER LIFE

One day, as per Rajmata's order on saying of Bodhidharman teacher, he sets out to leave for China.

After travelling the difficult journey of 3 years, Bodhidharman reached at Nanyang village, China.

As per the prediction by astrologers of there, a big danger was about to come in village.

When Bodhidharman reached at that village, the villagers assumed that he might be the danger.

The village started to disrespect him & tried to throw him out of the village. They began to shout- "Get Out, Get Out".

Bodhidharma left that village & villagers assumed danger has gone. But, the danger was about to come.

And, that danger came in form of dangerous epidemic disease of that 6th century- 'Bubonic Plague'- that spared no one.

But, Bodhidharma found the cure of that disease.

Villagers tried to throw the 1st infected body out of the village, the body was fully wrapped with bandages. But, Bodhidharma found that body and he took it into the cave with himself & treated that person & he succeed.

On the other hand, the disease was spreading all over the village.

When they saw, Bodhidharma treated that person, villagers began to address him as their God.

And then afterwards, Bodhidharma taught them the cure & began to treat other infected persons too & the whole situation began to correct.

Different doctors from across the world began to ask him the cure.

He taught them everything.

But the story didn't end there, after recovering from the epidemic disease, one more danger came into that village. But, that danger was in the disguise of humans.

Some warriors began to attack villagers, tried to kill them

But, Bodhidharma saved them.

According to villagers, Bodhidharma was only able to treat diseases, but they were not aware, that he was also an expert in Martial Arts, Self Defence & Empowering others.

Bodhidharma fought with them & saved all villagers.

People of China have never ever seen such art, and, they requested Bodhidharman to teach them, and, Bodhidharma taught them.

The people of China, began to call him Damu.

He stayed in that village, and, taught all his teachings to them.

After years passed by, when he desired to return to his native land, then the astrologers of that village told villagers to keep him to stay there, otherwise, on his return, the danger would come.

And, if they have to save themselves from danger, they have to stop him, whether he would be dead/alive.

The villagers added poison to his food to stop him.

But, Bodhidharma was very well aware about their plan, he told that to the villagers & agreed to eat that food. The villagers requested him that they want to bury his body in their village's land, that, only then, their village would be free of the danger.

Bodhidharma accepted their request, he ate that food & died at the age of 150 years.

The villagers buried his body in their village's land, buried on Mount Xionger to the west of Luoyang. but, his teachings were continued in China till now his teachings are growing in China.

And, he became the God for the People of China.

ZEN TEACHINGS OF BODHIDHARMA

'Zen' derives from Sanskrit word 'dhayan' meaning 'meditation.

It began with 6th Patriarch, Hui-neng (638-713).

Zen practices aim at taking the rational and intellectual mind out of the mental loop, so that students of Zen aim to achieve enlightenment by the way they live, and by mental actions that approach the truth without philosophical thought or intellectual endeavour.

Zen Buddhism is not a theory, or a body of knowledge. It's not a belief, a canon, or a religion; but rather, it's a practical experience.

Zen is not something you can intellelectualize, it's your personal experience of here & now.

Zen doesn't worry about after life, reincarnation, or God, it focus on the moment- right now.

Moreover, Zen accepts that human being is a mere mortal, who is incapable of answering the universe's impossible questions.

If we look deep into the Zen teachings, especially the Zen meditation, we would see that it is developed from Indian yoga- The Ashtanga yoga. In Ashtanga yoga, there are 8 steps to attain 'Samadhi'- the state in which you became divine, And, these 8 steps are-

1. Yama
2. Niyama
3. Asana
4. Pranayama
5. Pratayahara
6. Dharana

7. Dhyana
8. Samadhi

Zen Buddhism is branch of Mahayana Buddhism, that means, in actual, Zen created by Buddhist teachings combine with Indian yoga, for ex...let's see the sitting postures of Zen meditation, that actually taken from yoga.

Padmasana

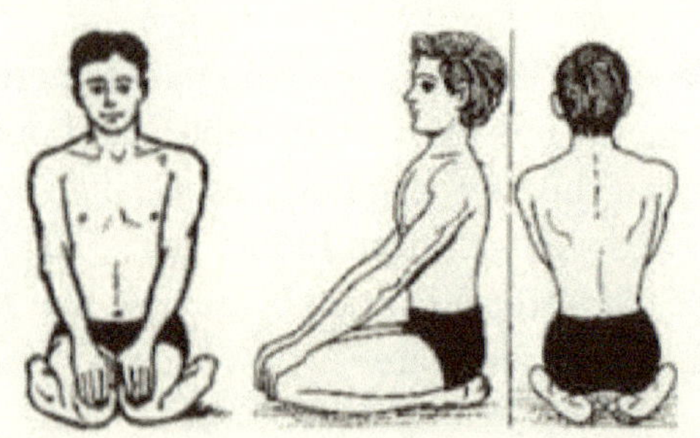

Vajrasana

Zen meditation, is combination of Pratayahara & Dharana. At the beginning of training of Zen practitioners, they try to avoid all kind of outside distractions and see oneself like a mirror, known as Pratayahara, then they train to not think of anything & fix your mind in nothingness, known as Dharana in yoga. It's now sure, that Indian yoga has great impact on Zen Buddhism.

Zen Meditation

At the core of Zen Buddhism is Zen Meditation or Zazen, meaning sitting. It is basically seated meditation wherein one practices in a good posture, pushing the sky, with the top of head, paying careful attention to breathing, until be fully alert & present. The end goal is to take someone's rational & intellectual mind out of the mental loop, so that he can realize his own Buddha nature.

The practice of Zen Meditation or Zazen is at the heart of Zen Buddhist experience. Originally, called Dhayan in India, Zen Meditation is a very simple yet precise method of meditation, where the correct posture is imperative, how, see below....

1. Find a quiet & peacefulplace where you will not be disturbed. The room where you will practice in should not be too dark or too bright, too warm or too cold.

2. Sit in lotus position, postures might seem uncomfortable & unnatural for most beginners, but with practice, your legs & hips will become more flexible, your mind will relax, & you will find posture to be quite comfortable. If the posture is too uncomfortable, try sitting in seiza- the traditional kneeling position used in Japan (and called Vajrasana in Yoga), for regular sitting in daily life. Keep your neck straight as possible and your tongue should be against the roof of your mouth just behind your teeth & traditionally, keep the eyes open during the meditation. Without focusing on nothing in particular, direct your vision, about one meter in front of you on the floor. Your eyes will naturally come to rest in a position that is half opened & half closed. The position of hands during Zazen is called cosmic mudra (see below image)- First, put your left hand on the right one, & palms turned towards the sky. Now, make an oval by touching the tips of thumbs together so that your thumbs touch each other. Both of your wrists should rest on your thighs; the edge of your hands should rest against your belly. Keep your shoulders relaxed.

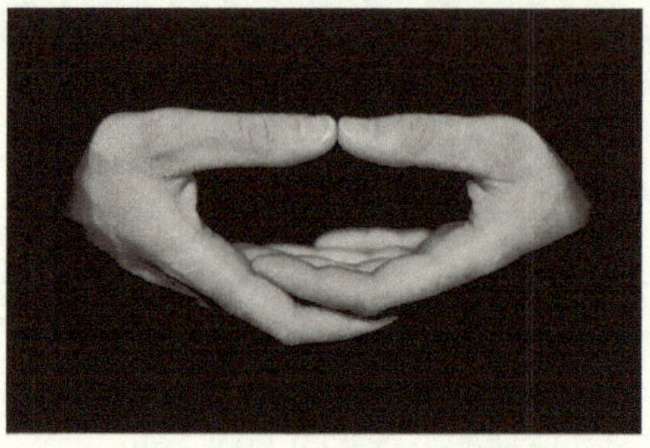

Cosmic Mudra

3. Breathing is the fundamental part of Zazen practice. Your breath should be deep long & natural and concentrate on breathing. As with the breathing, the mindset is essential in practice of Zen Meditation. The right state of mind emerges naturally from a deep concentration on posture & breathing. During Zazen, it's normal to have images, thoughts & emotions, coming up to the surface, appearing from unconscious mind. Do not pursue them or fight escape from them. The more you try to get rid of them, the more attention you give them, and the stronger they become. Try not to attach to them. Just let them go without judgement, like clouds in sky. So, as soon as you become aware that you are interacting or grasping on thoughts, immediately bring back your concentration to your posture & breathing your mind will settle down naturally. With experience, you will have less & less thoughts during Zazen, and your mind will come to rest more easily & more quickly.

4. Now, it's time to start Zazen. To avoid distraction, it's recommended that you practice facing a wall, as you would do in a training hall (dojo) or a monastery. Place your zafu (round cushion) on your zabuton (flat floor), so that, once sitting, your body is about one meter away from wall. If you are using a kneeling bench or a chair, also try to position yourself a meter away from the wall. Once you have finished Zazen, do gassho again- the Namaskar Mudra. Remain sitting on the cushion calmly & quietly for a few moments; don't hurry to stand up. Try not to talk for a few minutes after completing Zazen.

CHAPTER FIVE

SHAOLIN KUNG FU

Shaolin Kung Fu is one of the oldest martial arts after Kalaripayattu & it's the largest & most famous styles of Wushu or Kung Fu. Shaolin Kung Fu combines Zen Buddhism & Martial Arts together. Many people are under the impression that Kung Fu originated with the Shaolin Temple. It did not. Chinese Martial Arts were well developed in India before the Shaolin Temple was built. The temple was built in the 3rd century A.D.

30 years after Shaolin was founded, Bodhidharma came to China to teach Zen Buddhism. He travelled throughout China & finally came to Mt. Song where he found Shaolin Temple where he asked to be admitted. The abbot, Fang Chang, refused, and it is said Bodhidharma climbed high into the mountains to a cave where he meditated for 9 years. It is believed that he sat, facing the cave wall for much of these 9 years so that his shadow became permanently outlined on the cave wall. (Incidentally, the cave is now a sacred place & the shadow imprint has been removed from the cave & moved to the temple compound where you can view it during your visit. It is quite remarkable.) After 9 years, Fang Chang finally granted Bodhidharma entrance to Shaolin where he became the 1st Patriarch of Zen Buddhism. When he entered Shaolin Temple found that the monks there were not very fit. He introduced a series of exercises to them, that later became the foundation for specialized interpretation of Martial Arts at Shaolin.

The content of this training is given below-

1. Ye Gun Kung- Exercises designed to strengthen the physical body by working the tendons.
2. Sai Choi Kung- The art of cleansing the body-mind.
3. Sime Kung- Meditation practice incorporating: stationery or moving exercises training the practitioner to sense, improve & finally control

the movement of the Chi in his body; and spiritual training, an effort to directly perceive one's 'Original face' or 'Buddha Nature'. There are 3 exercises that given to Shaolin monks by Bodhidharma-

- The 18 Luohan Hands
- Sinew Metamorphosis
- Bone Marrow Cleansing

Over time, these fighting monks adapted the moves taught by Bodhidharma into early versions of Chinese Martial Arts techniques that developed through the early history of Shaolin into rudimentry forms of Kung Fu.

The 18 Luohan Hands

There is a famous saying, "all martial arts under heaven originated from Shaolin" and all styles at Shaolin originated from Luohan 18 hands & Luohanquan.

The word Luohan comes from the Sanskrit word Arhat. Both words refer to a person who has cultivated a high level of sprituality, after the Budhha passed away, 500 of his to disciples gathered together in a grand council.

Together, they reviewed & discussed his teachings word by word. these disciples became known as the 500 Arhats.

Bodhidharma while visiting the Shaolin Temple taught the monks a series of exercises based on Buddhist teachings, by observing & imitating the forms & expressions of Arhat statues in the temple, meditation & practice, those ancient exercises later evolved into a combat form called "18 hands of Luohan" (luohanshibashou), which is the oldest documented, systematized style of Shaolin Kung Fu.

According to the historical official text of Shaolin Temple, "Shaolin Kung Fu Manual" (shaoilnquanpu), in the Sui dynasty (581-618 AD). Shaolin monks had a selected set of 18 simple movements; until the Tang Dynasty (618-907 AD), the set had developed into 18 martial postures, that were combined into a form (taolu); the number of the postures increased to 36 until the early Song dynasty (960 AD); and in the Jin-Yuan dynasty (1115-1368 AD), it was developed into 173 movements; finally, in the Ming dynasty the system of the 18 hands of Luohan was completed in 18 forms, each form having 18 postures, making a total of 324 postures.

In Shaolin, this style is called "inborn Luohan's 18 hands" (xiantianluohan shibashou), because it was the style with which Shaolin king fu was born. Monk Shi Deqian, in his efforts to document Shaolin martial arts collected 8 forms of the 18 hands of Luohan into his "Encyclopedia of Shaolin martial arts". Of these forms, most lineages of Shaolin monks have mostly kept only one form, mostly the 1st, or the 8th form. Shaolin Luohan's 18 hands movements are simple & straight. The methods are mostly done by the palms of the hands. Fists, hook hands, and other hand gestures & kicks are less used.

Luohan's 18 hands are considered the elementary forms in Shaolin Kung Fu.

There is another Luohan's 18 hands style which is different from the original Shaolin Luohan's 18 hands but is more famous. This Luohan's 18 hands style has 18 different methods, consisted of 6 different methods of fist, 1 method of elbow, 2 methods of palm, 4 methods of leg, & 5 methods of joint locking. Of these 18 methods, a form of 24 movements for attack & defense is developed, which can be performed as a solo form or as a duet form. This style is originally from the Hua Quan style of Shangdong province & has later been adopted into Shaolin curriculum. Luohan Quan is considered a completely pure Buddhist Shaolin style. It is the most famous, & of the most important styles of Shaolin Kung fu. Shaolin monks developed Luohan Quan as an advanced style based on the 18 hands of Luohan. Luohan Quan has been created in the early ages of Shaolin Temple, but it was first officially documented by Shaolin monks in the "Shaolin Kung Fu Manual" in the early years of Song Dynasty in 960s AD. This style has two forms called small & big Luohan Quan, which are considered the oldest excellent styles of Shaolin Temple. There is a famous quote that Shaolin Luohan Quan has in total 108 different movements. Small Luohan Quan has 27 postures/36 movements & big Luohan Quan has about 54 postures/72 movements, so 108 movements in total. Big Luohan Quan is itself divided into 3 small 18-posture forms. Shi Deyang, 31st generation Shaolin monk talks about 6 forms of big Luohan Quan, but most people only know these 3 forms. The first 2 forms/sections of Big Luohan Quan, which has 36 postures in total, is an ancient form called golden child small Luohan Quan (jintongxiaoluohanquan). Shaolin small & big Luohan Quans are also practiced by the folk people of Dengfeng area around Shaolin in a less imitative version, which drops out or simplifies the Luohan imitating postures of Shaolin original Luohan Quan. Shaolin Luohan Quan movements, though simple, are highly advanced & deceptive. Attack & defence are masked by Luohan Buddhist postures & come out from unlikely angles.

During the centuries, Luohan Quan was developed. A major contribution was by monk Jue Yuan & two others named Li Sou & Bai Yufeng. Finally, as a result of the developements since the Jin & Yuan dynasties until the middle & late Ming dynasty, a Luohan Quan system of 18 forms was create, one form for each one of the famous Luohans, which at those times had increased in number to 18 in Chan Buddhism. In this style, each Luohan form is divided into 3 sections, so it has 54 sections in total. This style is less imitative than small & big Luohan Quan style & has given up or, at least, transformed many of the famous Luohan imitating postures. 18 Luohan Quan, though very famous, is rarely known. Even inside Shaolin, only a few people in each generation inherit this style completely. There are different versions of 18 Luohan Quan. One version has 18 forms for the 18 Luohans, while there are other versions with 9 long forms which altogether represent 18 Luohan characters. As an estimationof the diversity, just notice that Shaolin monk Shi Degen (1914-1970) taught 3 seemingly different versions to 3 of his disciples, Liu Zhenhai, Shi Yongwen, & Zhu Tianxi.

Because of it's long history, there are many versions of 18 Luohan Hands being taught today.

The Shaolin 18 Lohan Hands Qigoing Set

Yijin Jing (Sinew Metamorphosis) (Muscle Tendon Changing Classic)

It's a manual containing a series of exercises, coordinated with breathing, said to enhance physical health dramatically when practiced consistently. It's the mixture of Yoga & Kalaripayattu (an ancient Indian Martial Art from Kalari.) Kalaripayattu philosophy is Dharma- Yuddha (War of Truth). A Dharma Yuddha begins only if the fighter touches his Master's right hand with his right hand & his opponent chest & head. This move means that the fight can begin only through the mind & if only heart approved it. Maybe it's not a co-incidence that one of the 1st Shaolin Martial Arts named Xin Yi Quan (Heart through mind boxing).

In Chinese yi means "change", jin means "tendons & sinews", while jing means "methods". While some consider these exercises as a form of Qigong, it's a relatively intense form of exercise that aims at strengthening the muscles & tendons, so promoting strength & flexibility, speed & stamina, balance & co-ordination of the body. In the modern day, there are many translations & distinct sets of exercises all said to be derived from the original (the provenance of which is the subject of some debate). These exercises are notable for being a key element of the physical conditioning used in Shaolin training, The Yijin Jing was said to be left behind by Bodhidharma after his departure from the Shaolin Monastery, and discovered within his grave (or hidden in the walls of the temple) years after he had left. It was accompanied by another text, the XisuiJing, which was passed to a student of Bodhidharma's, but has not survived to the modern day. The monks of Shaolin supposedly practiced the exercises within the text but lost the true purpose of the document; Lin Buoyan recounts the legend that they "selfishely coveted it, practicing the skills therein, falling into heterodox ways, & losing the correct purpose of cultivating the Way".

Yi Jin Jing is a relatively intense form of exercise that aims at strengthening the muscles & tendons, so promoting strength & flexibility, speed & stamina, balance & co-ordination of the body. The Yi Jin Jing taught the Shaolin Monks how to build their internal energy to an abundant level & use it to improve health & change their physical bodies from weak to strong. After the Monks practiced the Yi Jin Jing exercises, they found that not only did they improve their health, but also they also greatly increased their strength. When this training was in integrated into the martial arts forms, it increased their martial techniques. This change marked one more step in the growth of Shaolin Martial Arts. The Shaolin monks have made some fame for themselves through their fighting skill; this is all due to having obtained this manuscript. Both documents were written in an Indian language which was not well understood by the monks of the temple. According to one legend, a monk decided that the text must contain more valuable knowledge, then simply self defense, and went on a pilgrimage with a copy of the text to find someone who could translate the deeper meaning of the text. He eventually met an Indian priest named Pramati in the province of Szechwan who, examining the text, explained that the meaning of the text was extraordinally deep & beyond his ability to translate fully. He nonetheless provided a partial translation. The monk found that within a year of practicing the techniques as Pramati had translated, that his constitution had become "as hard as steel", and he felt that he could be a Buddha. The monk was so pleased that he thereafter followed Pramati wherever he went.

The number of exercises tends to change; some contend that 18 should be the correct one (if based on 18 Arhats), but can vary from 10 to 24, to 30. Today, most respected routine is that of Wang Zuyuan, composed of 12 exercises, & has been adopted by the Academics of Chinese Medicine in China. Chang Renxia together with Chang Weizhen proposed an alternative set of 14 exercises, which can be of interest for the therapeutic effects he promises. Deng Mingdao presents a version with 24 exercises, but with another name, Xisui Jing.

In fact, another point of contention is the relationship between Xisui Jing & Yijin Jing. Some authors tend to use those 2 names for the same routine; others keep things seperated & invoke different results & different effects on the body. The 12 Posture Moving Exercise kept to this day is something that Wang Zuyuan learned at Shaolin Monastery on Mount Song. It is somewhat different from the original "Picture of stationery exercise" & the "Guide to the art of attack" (as Guangdong sources demonstrate). The 12 Posture Moving Exercise supposedly describes what is called the purported "12 fists of Bodhidharma" in many Southern Martial Arts, most notably Hung Gar & Wing Chun. Legend states that the 12 exercises were developed based on the movements of 12 animals that Bodhidharma studied after his 9 years of Meditation. These exercises aided the health of Shaolin

Monastery Monks, & contributed to many of the animal based Martial Arts in China. The basic purpose of Yijin Jingis to turn flaccid & frail sinews & tendons into strong & sturdy ones. The movements of Yijin Jingare at once vigorous & gentle. Their performance calls for a unity of will & strength, i.e. using one's will to direct exertion of muscular strength. It is coordinated with breathing. Better muscles & tendons means better health & shape, more resistance, flexibility, & endurance.

According to an ancient book from Song Dynasty, the spirit can be improved if you practice the method continiously.

- The 1st year of training gives back physical & mental vitality.
- The 2nd year enhances blood circulation & nurtures merridians.
- The 3rd year allows flexibility to muscles & nurtures the organs.
- The 4th year improves meridians & nurtures viscera.
- The 5th year washes the marrow & nurtures the brain.

The 5 rules of Yijin Jingare:-

- Quietness- like lake water reflects the moon, a calm spirit allows energy to move inside the body.
- Slowness- in order to use & flex muscles deeply, to get maximum extension & move Qi & Xue, slow movements are required.
- Extension- each movement must be brought to the maximum.
- Pause- efficacy comes through waiting & keeping tension for a longer time.
- Flexibility- limbs & trunks must be extended so that blood & energy can circulate, so we have flexiblity.

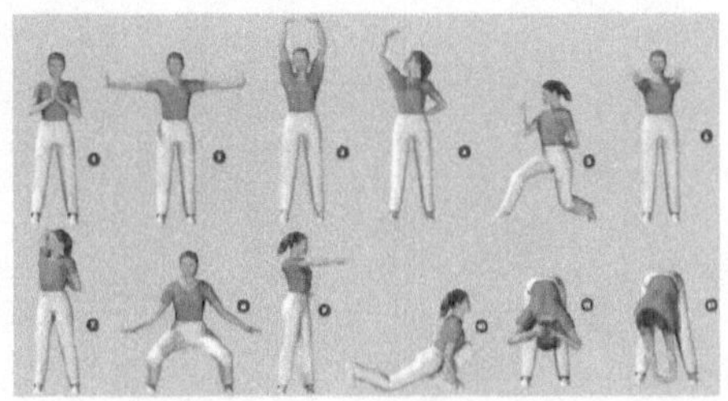

Sinew Metamorphosis

Bone Marrow Cleansing (Xi Sui Jing)

Bone marrow cleansing (Xi Sui Jing) is the 3rd Chi Kung Treasure taught by the Great Bodhidharma in the Shaolin Temple. Unlike to the 18 Luohan Hands & the 12 exercises of Sinew Metamorphosis, there are no pictures & records on how Bone Marrow Cleansing was practiced in the Shaolin Temple. In contrast to the 2 sets of exercises we interpret Bone Marrow Cleansing as a master's skill without physical outward form.

CHAPTER SIX

FIVE ELEMENTS

Everything in nature is made up of five basic elements: earth, water, fire, air, and space. Knowledge of the five elements allows the yogi to understand the laws of nature and to use yoga to attain greater health, power, knowledge, wisdom and happiness. This arises out of deep intuition of how the universe operates.

EARTH

1. Mountain Pose (Tadasana)

TADASANA

2. Warrior I Pose (Virabhadrasana 1)

VIRBHADRASANA

3. Tree Pose (Vrikshasana)

VRIKSHASANA

4. Eagle Pose (Garudasana)

GADUDASANA

5. Head-to-Knee Forward Bend (Janu Sirsasana)

JANU SIRASANA

6. Hero Pose (Virasana)

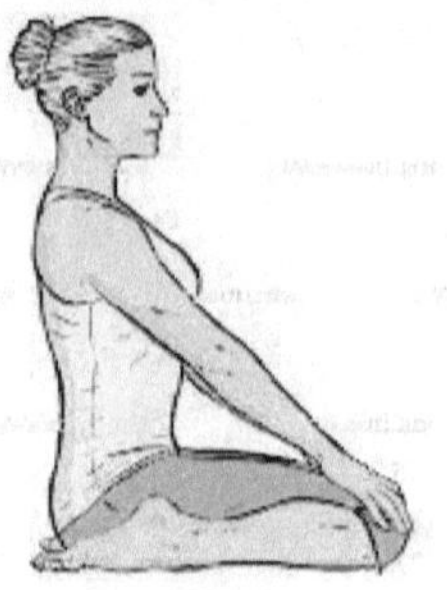

VIRASANA

7. Child's Pose (Balasana)

BALASANA

8. Corpse Pose (Savasana)

SAVASANA

WATER

1. Cobra Pose

COBRA POSE

2. Dog Pose

DOG POSE

3. LOW LUNGE POSE

LOW LUNGE POSE

4. Bound Angle Pose (Badhakonasana)

BADHKONASANA

5. Frog Pose (Mandukasana)

MANDUKASANA

6. Pigeon Pose (Eka Pada Rajakapotasan)

EKA PADA RAJAKAPOTASANA

7. Bridge Pose (Setu Bandhasana)

BRIDGE POSE

8. Happy Baby Pose (Ananda Balasana)

ANANDA BALASANA
HAPPY BABY POSE

ANAND BALASANA

9. Visualization Meditation

Take a comfortable seat and close your eyes. Take a few deep, cleansing breaths to center before beginning the meditation.

Visualize yourself diving into a body of water—it could be the ocean, a lake, or a pool—whatever comes to you first. As you dive in, notice how the water feels on your face and on your skin.

Notice the temperature of the water and the sensations you feel as you dive deeper into the water. Watch yourself continue to dive deeper and deeper and deeper. Pay attention to how it feels to keep diving deeper into the water.

Then you start to ascend and come up to the surface for just enough time to get a deep breath of air, then you dive back in. Repeat this cycle several times in your mind—surfacing, breathing, and descending again.

After a few minutes or when you feel ready to get out of the water, start to surface again, this time finding your way to dry land.

Notice your transition of slowly getting out of the water: The cool air hitting your skin, the cool earth under your feet. As you walk, notice any sounds, smells, or tastes.

Notice the sun showing up to warm you up—your face, your arms, your entire body—to dry you off.

When you're completely dry, bring awareness back to your breath, slow inhales and exhales through the nose.

FIRE

1. Sun Salutation (Surya Namaskar)

SURYA NAMASKAR

2. Plank Pose (Phalakasana)

PHALAKASANA

3. Tiger Pose (Vyaghrasana)

VYAGHRASANA

4. Revolved Lunge Pose (Parivrtta Anjaneyasana)

PARIVRTTA ANJANEYASANA

5. Chair Pose (Utkatasana)

CHAIR POSE

6. Boat Pose (Navasana)

NAVASANA

7. Half Lord of the Fishes Pose (Ardha Matsyendrasana)

ARDH MATSYENDRASANA

AIR

1. Easy Pose (Sukhasana)

Sukhasana

2. Cobra Pose (Bhujangasana)

BHUJANGASANA

3. Cow/Cat Pose (Bitilasana/Marjaryasana)

COW/CAT POSE

4. Bow Pose (Dhanurasana)

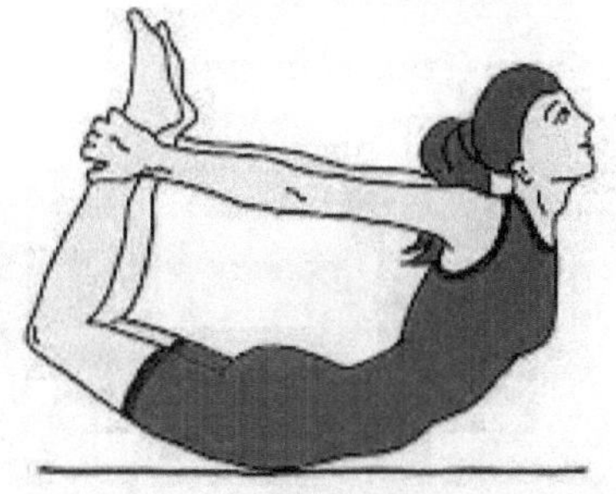

DHANURASANA

6. Camel Pose (Ustrasana)

USTRASANA

7. Lord of the Dance Pose (Natarajasana)

NATARAJASANA

SPACE

1. Lion Pose (Simhasana)

SIMHASANA

2. Star Pose (Utthita Tadasana)

UTTHITA TADASANA

3. Camel Pose (Ustrasana)

USTRASANA

4. Fish Pose (Matsyasana)

MATSYASANA

5. Shoulder Stand (Salamba Sarvangasana)

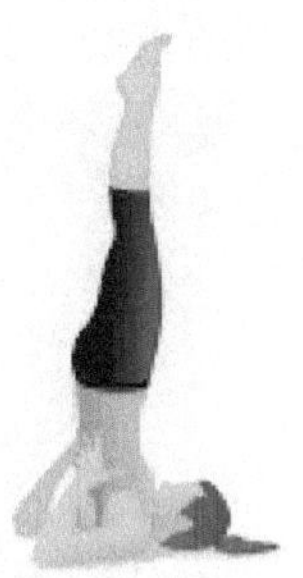

SALAMBA SARVANGASANA

6. Legs Up the Wall Pose (Viparita Karani)

VIPARITA KARANI

7. Corpse Pose (Savasana)

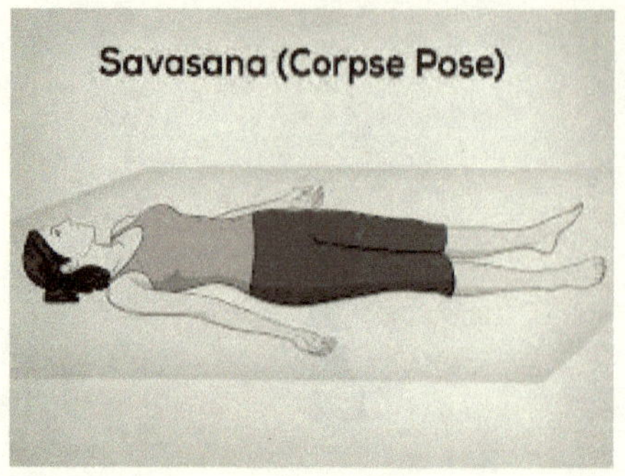

SAVASANA

HYPNOSIS

Hypnosis is a changed state of awareness and increased relaxation that allows for improved focus and concentration. It is also called hypnotherapy. Hypnosis usually is done with the guidance of a health care provider using verbal repetition and mental images. During hypnosis, most people feel calm and relaxed .

Why it's done?

Hypnosis can be an effective way to cope with stress and anxiety. In particular, it may ease stress and anxiety before a medical procedure, such as a breast biopsy.

Hypnosis also may be helpful for:

- **Pain control.** Hypnosis may help with pain due to burns, cancer, childbirth, irritable bowel syndrome, fibromyalgia, jaw problems, dental procedures and headaches.
- **Hot flashes.** Hypnosis may ease hot flashes caused by menopause.
- **Behavior change.** Hypnosis has been used with some success to treat sleep problems, bed-wetting, smoking and overeating.
- **Cancer treatment side effects.** Hypnosis has been used to ease side effects from chemotherapy and radiation treatment.
- **Mental health conditions.** Hypnosis may help reduce anxiety associated with fears and phobias.

What type of person can be hypnotized?

Hypnosis can work for almost anyone, though some people have an easier time than others. If you're lucky, you'll be one of the few people (about 5 to 10 percent of the population) who is highly susceptible to hypnotic suggestion.

What are the risks of hypnosis?

Hypnosis is considered to be a safe treatment when performed by a qualified and experienced practitioner. In rare cases, however, a patient may have unwanted side effects such as: Dizziness. Headache.

Can hypnosis change a person?

Hypnotherapy can not change habits and beliefs that you would never change, nor can it completely change who you are. Because Hypnosis works with your mind and your thoughts, feelings and emotions it can only enhance what is already there and not make a total new person.

SYMPTOMS:

However, it's commonly believed that in the deep state of focus and relaxation that's achieved with hypnosis: Your conscious mind is quieted. You're able to tap into the part of your brain where your thoughts, beliefs, perceptions, sensations, emotions, memory and behaviors originate.

Body

The muscles relax, and the subject makes efforts to become more comfortable. A person in hypnosis does not remain physically tense. Muscular relaxation is often most noticeable in the facial expression. A person in hypnosis has a smooth, ironed out expression on the face, which usually goes along with a vacant look in the eyes.

Stillness. A person does not have to be frozen still to experience trance, but a person in hypnosis does not make restless movements such as hand wringing or foot shaking, for example. Even people who normally experience tics or twitches do not usually manifest them while in hypnosis. When a person in trance does move, they will be slow and efficient in their movements.

Body warmth is frequently an indication of hypnosis.

Eyes

A person entering trance begins to blink more slowly.

Fluttering of the eyelids occurs during the initial phase of trance. This is one sign of hypnosis that cannot be imitated.

The eyes sometimes roll upward, so that you see only the whites of the eyes.

Increased lacrimation (watering of the eyes).

In hypnosis there is often a reddening of the eyes.

Though not observable outwardly, a person in trance often reports fogging or blurring of the vision. Hypnosis can also cause tunnel vision, or even changes in the colors, sizes, and shapes of things.

Attention

A person in hypnosis will be less distracted by outside sounds. To the extreme, the subject may become so inwardly absorbed that he or she no longer make the effort to listen to the hypnotherapist.

Pulse and respiration

Pulse rate and breathing slow down, although sometimes a person entering hypnosis will experience a temporary increase in pulse and respiration caused by the realization that they are in hypnosis.

Swallowing

The swallowing reflex slows or disappears during trance. Of course, if attention is drawn to it, the subject will usually swallow.

Psychomotor retardation

There is often a lag of time between the time when a suggestion is given and when the subject in hypnosis carries it out.

Signs of reorientation

When the feet and hands begin touching each other restlessly it is a good sign that the subject is exiting trance. Other signs of a person reorienting themselves to the body and the waking state are wetting the lips, shifting the posture, opening the eyes, blinking, yawning, and stretching.

Meditation and self-hypnosis

Many of the common instructions for meditation and relaxation imitate the signs of hypnosis. Here is a very simple checklist of things you can do to facilitate meditation and trance states.

Make sure you are not cold.

Find a comfortable position.

Be still. If you must move, do it slowly and efficiently.

Relax your body, especially your face.

With your eyes open, stare at something slightly below eye level. Notice the loss of detail in objects in your peripheral vision.

Roll your eyes upward gently.

When you cannot keep your eyes open any longer, close your eyes and relax them.

HYPNOTHERAPY IN PSYCHIATRY

What Is Hypnotherapy?

Hypnotherapy is an adjunctive technique that utilizes hypnosis to aid in the treatment of specific symptoms or health conditions. Hypnotherapy works by inducing a hypnotic state marked by waking awareness that allows people to experience detached external attention and to focus on inner experiences.

It is sometimes used as part of a treatment plan for phobias and other anxiety disorders. It is also sometimes used for pain management, weight loss, smoking cessation, and a variety of other applications.

Formal explorations in the therapeutic uses for hypnosis began in the late 1700s but did not gain scientific credibility until much more recently. Modern researchers have further explored how hypnosis can be used, which conditions it can treat, and how effective it may be compared to other treatments.

What Hypnotherapy Can Help With?

There are many different reasons why a person might want to try hypnotherapy. Research suggests that some possible applications include:

- Chronic pain conditions
- Dementia symptom
- Nausea and vomiting related to chemotherapy
- Pain during childbirth, dental procedures, or surgery
- Skin conditions, such as psoriasis and warts
- Symptoms of irritable bowel syndrome (IBS)
- Symptoms of attention-deficit/hyperactivity disorder (ADHD)

Hypnotherapy may also be used by licensed physicians and psychologists in the treatment of conditions like anxiety disorders, depression, eating disorders, and post-traumatic stress disorder (PTSD).

Hypnotherapy may also be helpful for changing or reducing problematic behaviors. Because of this, it is sometimes used to help people quit smoking, lose weight, and sleep better.

Benefits of Hypnotherapy

Some people may experience dramatic results with hypnotherapy. In other cases, people may simply feel very relaxed. Some of the benefits of hypnotherapy may include:

Awareness: Some people remain fully aware during the entire experience. They recall everything that happens and are even able to have conversations while under hypnosis. Other people may experience states of relaxation that are so deep that they may even feel detached from what is happening.

Focus: Most of the time, we are distracted by our surroundings. Whether the TV is blaring, your kids are demanding attention or your spouse wants to talk, it can be difficult to fully focus on yourself. Our conscious minds are also cluttered. You may be worried about paying a bill, concerned about an upcoming project, or planning tonight's dinner. The therapy session is intended to break through these day-to-day concerns and allow you to focus completely on the problem at hand.

Relaxation: In the hypnotic state, you are deeply relaxed. Your conscious mind is quieted, allowing your unconscious mind to deeply focus on your issue. You are also calmer, and therefore more receptive to facing your problems or fears.

Most hypnotherapists utilize a series of calming messages, such as "you are safe" and "no one can harm you" to reassure their clients that during hypnosis they can objectively face their problems without having a panicked reaction.

Effectiveness

The effectiveness and impact of hypnotherapy can vary based on the individual and how the treatment is used. Hypnotherapy has been shown to have some degree of efficacy for certain applications, particularly:

Pain reduction and control during dental procedures and childbirth

Reduction in nausea and vomiting in individuals being treated for cancer with chemotherapy

Reduction in the severity of symptoms associated with irritable bowel syndrome (IBS)4

While it may help people cope with problems related to stress and anxiety, it may be best applied when used in conjunction with first-line treatments such as cognitive behavioral therapy (CBT) and medications.

The results of a study published in the May 2021 issue of the Journal of Affective Disorders found that hypnotherapy was not less effective than CBT for treating mild to moderate depression. The results indicated that where CBT led to a 38.5% reduction in symptom severity, hypnotherapy resulted in a 44.6% reduction.

As researchers continue to explore the potential uses for hypnotherapy, this technique may gain greater acceptance in the treatment of various conditions.

Special Quotes By Bodhidharma

1) "NOT THINKING ABOUT ANYTHING IS ZEN, ONCE YOU KNOW THIS, WALKING, SITTING OR LYING DOWN, EVERYTHING YOU DO IS ZEN"

2) "TO SEEK IS TO SUFFER, TO SEEK NOTHING IS BLISS"

3) "BUT PEOPLE OF THE DEPPEST UNDERSTANDING LOOK WITHIN, DISTRACTED BY NOTHING, SINCE A CLEAR MIND IS THE BUDDHA, THEY ATTAIN THE UNDERSTANDING OF BUDDHA, WITHOUT USING THE MIND"

4) "THOSE WHO WORSHIP, DON'T KNOW, AND, THOSE WHO KNOW DON'T WORSHIP"

5) "AT EVERY MOMENT, WHERE LANGUAGE CAN'T GO, THAT'S YOUR MIND"

6) "POVERTY & HARDSHIP ARE CREATED BY FALSE THIMKING"

7) "ACCORDING TO SUTRAS, EVIL DEEDS RESULT IN HARDSHIPS, &, GOOD DEEDS RESULT IN BLESSINGS"

8) "ALL KNOW THE WAY, FEW ACTUALLY WALK IT"

9) "NOT ENGAGING IN IGNORANCE IS WISDOM"

10) "VAST EMPTINESS, NOTHING HOLY"

11) "EVERYTHING SACRED, NOTHING SACRED"

12) "PEOPLE OF THIS WORLD ARE DELUDED, THEY ARE ALWAYS LONGING FOR SOMETHING, ALWAYS, IN A WORD, SEEKING"

13) "AS BUDDHA IS SOMEONE, WHO FINDS FREEDOM, IN GOOD FORTUNE & BAD"

14) "BUDDHA IS AN IDLE PERSON, HE DOESN'T RUN AROUND, AFTER FORTUNE & FAME"

15) "REGARDLESS OF WHAT WE DO, OUR KARMA HAS NO HOLD ON US"

16) "BUDDHA MEANS AWARENESS, AWARENESS OF BODY & MIND, THAT PREVENTS EVIL, FROM ARISING IN EITHER'

17) "THE IGNORANT MIND, WITH ITS INFINITE AFFLICTIONS, PASSIONS & EVILS, IS ROOTED IN THREE POISONS, GREED, ANGER & DELUSION"

18) "FEELING ONESELF FROM WORDS, IS LIBERATION"

19) "IF YOU USE YOUR MIND TO STUDY REALITY, YOU WON'T UNDERSTAND, EITHER YOUR MIND OR REALITY, IF YOU STUDY

REALITY WITHOUT USING YOUR MIND, YOU WILL UNDERSTAND BOTH"

20) "THE WAY IS BASICALLY PERFECT, IT DOESN'T REQUIRE PERFECTING"

www.ingramcontent.com/pod-product-compliance
Lightning Source LLC
Chambersburg PA
CBHW031429160726
47993CB00003B/1470